# Turning Adversaries into Allies in the Workplace

## Lila G. Roomberg

Peter
This may not be deathless
prose, but you should
get a laugh or two out of it.
Lila

### VANTAGE PRESS
New York

To Jessica and Timothy

# Contents

# Preface

My qualifications for writing this book are the experiences gained over fifty years of doing a wide variety of jobs. They ranged from payroll clerk in a very efficient necktie factory in New York's garment industry to partner in a prestigious law firm. In the course of a lifetime working with and for others, I finally learned how to do it. I will try to shorten the process for you. But first a word about work in general.

As I reviewed other writings on the general subject of work, I was appalled to discover that most of them dealt with work as if it were a damn nuisance that could be avoided without risk and ofttimes with enormous advantage. These writings also implied that all bosses were demented and should be finessed, if not ignored; that all co-workers were lazy or ignorant, or both; and that nothing could be done about either of them.

I assume that these writings are meant to be amusing. Sorry, my friends, but the subject is not funny. The advice given in these so-called works of humor is unreliable if believed and potentially perilous to one's economic health if taken seriously. *Conduct Expected: The Unwritten Rules for a Successful Business Career,* by William Lareau, New Century Publishers, Inc., 1985, is an exception. The author tells the plain truth in warning that there is no easy way to be a success in this world without a lot of boring, mundane, difficult, and often disgusting and humiliating work alongside of people who cannot remember your name. To this I would add that the ladder to success includes sleepless nights over stomach-wrenching problems, soul-searing mistakes, paralyzing decisions, bouts of dry mouth, and periods of sweaty palms. That is just the way it is. Face it and understand that you are not alone.

What was more surprising, to me at least, was the notion that work should be fun, uplifting, fascinating, and above all soothing. I am particularly annoyed when I hear pundits say: "The right thing will come along when you are ready."

To this I say, if I waited until I was ready, I would never get out of bed.

Or here's another one: "When your job is no longer any fun, it is time to quit."

Again I ask, since when was fun a part of the job description?

The approach that I have taken is that since we must work to support ourselves, our dependents, and our constantly expanding list of needs, we might as well do it well and with as much good humor as we can muster. It certainly doesn't cost any more in time or money. This advice will probably strike some folks as quaint and completely out of touch. But there is no harm in it, and it might help. You can't say that about many other ideas.

Face it. Work is just that—WORK. Done right, it is still generally hard. There is really no use pretending that it is or should be something else. Get it done without troubling too many people in the process and maybe, just maybe, it will give you, besides your living, a certain sense of satisfaction.

Much of what you will read here will sound familiar. This is not surprising. You probably heard some of it from others, and a great deal of it has been in the back of your own head all the time. Still relevant after more than sixty years is *How to Win Friends and Influence People,* by Dale Carnegie. Read it if only to convince yourself that people really do not change.

This book contains practical solutions that will help you avoid error, wasted energy, and disappointment. The suggestions, ideas, and tools are general enough to be adapted to almost any work environment.

A dear friend of mine always insists that her latest find (the newest gadget, theory, or spa) will change my life. This small book will not change your life, but it will demonstrate how a few simple techniques can help you manage everyday workplace frustrations. You should find at least a few useful strategies. If you know of others, please share them. There is a real need here. Talk shows, books, and magazines are full of advice about your sex life, but are almost devoid of help about your work life. This appears to be odd since I assume that most of us spend more time on the latter pursuit than the former.

# Acknowledgments

The help of my daughter, Virginia Simon, made much of this book possible. She can find any information and is mostly responsible for the guidance given in Chapter IX. Many thanks are more than due to Jamie Bischoff for her help and encouragement. But nothing would have been started without the nagging from John Williams.

Illustrations by Robert Biancalana, Mill Valley, California
Photograph by Michael Ahearn, Philadelphia, Pennsylvania
Cover Design by Louis J. Forgione

# I

# Work

**Definitions:**

Work: ". . . the labor, task, or duty that is one's accustomed means of livelihood . . ."

Play: ". . . recreational activity . . . absence of serious or harmful intent . . . to engage in sport or recreation . . . to engage or take part in a game . . . to perform or execute for amusement . . . to perform (music) on an instrument . . ."

Avocation: ". . . a subordinate occupation pursued in addition to one's vocation, especially for enjoyment . . ."

Vocation: ". . . the work in which a person is regularly employed."[1]

VOCATION                    AVOCATION

1. *Webster's Ninth New Collegiate Dictionary.* Merriam-Webster Inc., 1984.

1

Please study these definitions carefully. Many people confuse work with play and vocation with avocation. Too many of them seem to think that those concepts are somehow the same. And to their regret—and many times to their economic peril—they find that this isn't so.

*Avocation* comes from the Latin, meaning "to call away." *Vocation* comes from the Latin, meaning "to call to." That should give you a hint as to the difference between the two concepts.

Put another way, you should not expect someone to pay you (complete with benefits that may add another 30 to 40 percent) for doing what you like to do or even what you do very well. Though you love playing the harp, the number of people who are willing and able to pay to hear you may be somewhat limited, as may be those who wish to follow in your footsteps and pay to be taught.

Here is where the difference between vocation and avocation comes in: one is your day job, and the other is your leisure-time pursuit. A vocation adds to your purse; an avocation adds to your life. But unless you are among the very few who possess great talent, a lot of luck, and a rich relative or spouse, an avocation will never substitute for a vocation.

An avocation is what makes a complete life. It can open doors to you and fill your time with interesting people. Golfers often play for the companionship as well as for the exercise. Bridge is a wonderful way to meet people when on vacation or in a new town. But hobbies aren't nearly as much fun when that is all you have to do.

None of this is meant to convey the notion that your vocation, or your job, is meant to be constant drudgery. Once you begin to do a thing well, you may find yourself falling in like, if not in love. The key to liking your work is doing it well. Doing it well means knowing how to do it, and, just as important, how to work with other people.

It should come as no shock to discover that there are few shortcuts in this business of work, although we constantly seek

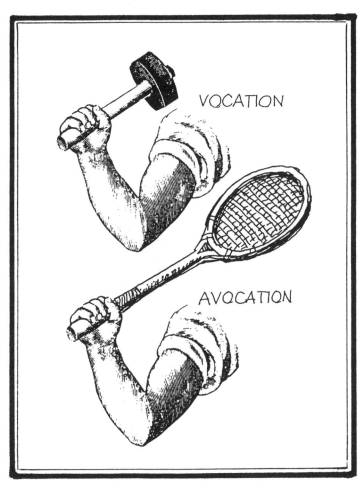

VOCATION

AVOCATION

them. Work is a lot like dieting. It never ends. You can cheat once in a while with a banana split, but eat one every day and you are sure to lose sight of your weight goal. In this same context, inattention to your work is like eating a banana split. If you keep allowing this tempting distraction to come into your work on a daily basis, you will not only lose sight of your work goal; you may also lose your job.

To avoid this job loss, you need to rid yourself of the distractions—the banana splits—by building a strong relationship with your work. This process is similar to building a personal relationship. In a personal relationship, you find out all you can about a person and try your best to please him or her. In a relationship with work, you learn all you can about the work and then strive to meet and maybe exceed the requirements for that work. Like all good relationships, familiarity is not synonymous with boredom. In fact, in a relationship with work, familiarity breeds fondness rather than contempt.

There is no occupation or profession that does not have experts (and no-so-experts) writing about it. When I started law school, no one had a clue as to what all those cases meant or how to study the material. The very good advice that we received was just to plunge in, swim around as fast as possible, and hopefully, by the end of the first year, most of it would make some sense. This proved true, and I recommend this method when you begin a new job or line of work. In other words—just get started. You cannot just sit around until someone bumps into you. Learn as much as you can before you report to work on that first day. Some preliminary investigative work should give you some idea of the product or service involved, the players, and the general environment.

Once you have a general idea of what is before you, it is time to be more discriminating about your studies. Focus in on what you need to know now. Focus in on what your work requires now. Taking the time to learn about the work as a whole and what your responsibilities are within that whole, will help you understand and conquer the concept of work.

For some, work conjures up images of power and glamour. Others see work as everyday drudgery. But no matter how you cut it, work is just what it sounds like—work. At times, work provides ample satisfaction. Other times, it is a source of frustration. You can experience a sense of relief or accomplishment when a task is completed. You may even feel a sense of exhilaration knowing you finished a job that you thought you couldn't do. These moments of high emotion should never be forgotten. Remember and treasure them.

The point here is not to expect your work to be fun and games, your boss to be your pal, your employer to be your mother, your office to be your home, or your co-workers to be your friends or lovers. What you should expect and work towards is adequate compensation and a healthy environment in which to function.

What you should get is satisfaction from a job well done and enough money to support yourself and those who rely on you. If this is not occurring, it may be time to move on See chapter III—"When to Hold and When to Fold."

Now that I have you thoroughly depressed, here is the good news. All around you are people, people who will help you if you know how to proceed. Think of yourself as the ugly duckling who discovers that he/she is really a swan and glides through the water of the world with all the other swans.

All those people who you thought were out to get you, make you look bad and stupid or foolish, can help you in ways that you and they never even imagined. They may not be your friends, but you need not make them enemies. You need them and they need you, whether you know it or not. They have information, contacts, skills, and much more that you can use without resort to either bribery or extortion—just some smarts. I promise.

"This is what we call the playpen."

# II

# How to Get Others to Cooperate

It is important to understand that what you are doing at this very moment may be of little consequence to those on whom you must rely for cooperation. In most situations your part of the project may be dependent upon the cooperation or input of others. Somehow you must instill in those around you the same sense of urgency that you feel about the job at hand. There are several ways that you can do this, or at least increase the odds (always against you) that those upon whom you depend will do everything they are supposed to do. They will bring the right papers; they will make sure the food is brought in on time; they will make all those calls; they will pick up the packages or children; they will write the report or letter, they will have the right people at the right place; and they will make sure nobody walks off in a huff.

Here's how.

**Make it as easy as possible for the other party to perform the assigned task.**

Big business is usually good at this. They use self-addressed envelopes, sometimes with postage prepaid. They install 800 numbers to encourage you to buy their products or contribute to their causes. They insert self-addressed, postage-prepaid reply cards in magazines and newspapers. I should warn you that there seems to be a growing backlash against these. One writer, obviously annoyed with the number of postcards falling in his lap, advised his readers to send them back, either blank or with a cheery, but anonymous, message. Not all of these may be applicable to your work, but you can keep in mind the principle.

Some other ways you can make life a bit easier for others and increase their willingness to cooperate with you are:

1. Highlight, tab, or flag signature lines and areas which someone has to fill in and make sure you have left enough room to provide the information. I hate those forms that just tell me to attach a second sheet if I need more room.

2. Unless the prize is a full scholarship to an Ivy League college, keep your questionnaire to one page, and please don't ask me for any essay. If I want to answer with more than yes, no, or maybe, I will write you a letter.

3. Organize your thoughts and papers before asking for another's cooperation. It is too easy to finesse your request if someone can find a single meaningless part.

4. It is not necessary to give any reasons for your request unless specifically asked. It just confuses the situation and sets you up for an argument about justification.

5. Be pleasant and very matter-of-fact. If they think that world peace is at stake, they might get nervous.

6. Provide a deadline—preferably before you really need it.

An hour's worth of thought and preparation at the beginning will save you days of aggravation at the end and may even avoid a disaster.

**Do not be timid about repeating instructions.**

Repeating instructions already given by telephone or letter is a courtesy, not an annoyance. It does not constitute nagging, which is an entirely different resource and is covered later on.

The story is often told about the preacher who said that first he tells the congregation what he is going to tell them. Then he tells them what he wants to tell them, and finally, he tells them what he just told them. This was his way of getting his message across.

Do what the preacher does. Be absolutely clear. Leave no room for doubt or alternative interpretations. I found the preacher's advice particularly helpful when organizing multistage projects, even settlements of transactions that required in attendance several people (sometimes dozens of people) who each brought with them at least one lawyer and a long list of conditions which must be met before they would sign or pay any money.

No matter what the situation, directions are needed to carry you through it. And the more explicit your directions, the better off you are.

First, call the person who may need directions and explain what must be done and why. Inform the other party that no notes need be taken now because your call will be followed up by a detailed written communication. At this point you should hear a sigh of relief, if not gratitude. It is essential that your follow-up communication be absolutely the same as the telephoned one to avoid any arguments later on. The only way to do this is to have your screen or paper in front of you when calling. Send these instructions by e-mail or fax very soon after the telephone call before the other party forgets what the whole thing is about and assumes that the message was intended for someone else.

Of course, you will apologize for all the detail, but I have never known anyone who was offended by step-by-step directions.

Clear, concise directions are especially important for people who are traveling to get to you. It's not enough to tell someone how to get somewhere; you should also specify the best roads and the location of parking garages or lots. Those traveling by train or plane could use some welcome hints about taxis, public transportation, and available hotel accommodations.

Take it upon yourself to become familiar with the train and plane schedules to your city. Keep a stock of hotel brochures. You can get them from any travel agent. Establish a nodding acquaintance with a hotel manager. This could be helpful in emergencies. The name of the game is preparation.

After all the telephone calls and written instructions, do not assume that all is well. It is not. It is absolutely necessary to take the next step. Call a few days before the event is to take place and confirm everything. Never, never rely on e-mail or unreturned telephone answering messages. Speak to someone, preferably over the age of consent. Getting an answer sometimes takes a bit of maneuvering. You will need all your skill and perseverance, especially if you are asking for a decision.

## When You Need Them to Make Up Their Minds

Try making the act of decision-making as painless as possible. I have often sent notes with some suggested answers. It doesn't always work, but once again I have improved the odds.

May I have your permission to . . .

&#9633; Yes
&#9633; No
&#9633; Let's talk about this on . . .
&#9633; Call me next . . .
&#9633; Ask Mr./Ms./Mrs. . . .

This is the situation as I see it . . .

There are three options:
1. —
2. —
3. —
(I agree with No _____/You decide/None of the above/See me tomorrow.)

The variations are endless and humor helps. Use your imagination and adapt the suggested answers to the subject. If you are gifted that way, amusing drawings or rhymes are helpful and will get you noticed. If you're not, check out the wide variety of Post-it and other note pads. They are very clever and show that you do not take yourself too seriously. Don't be afraid of being a bit outrageous, but symbols denoting gender are far too commonplace for this purpose. If all else fails, see chapter VIII—"Nagging."

Sometimes a simple yes or no is not enough. The issues are a bit more complicated. The same general approach can be used. Remember, though, at this point you probably know more about the issue than anyone else. What you need is guidance.

Before you go in to see the decision-maker, give some notice about the subject. No one likes surprises or being put on a spot. Give the facts, issues, risks, rewards, and most of all your solution and reasons for coming to the conclusion. Never sit back and say "What shall I do?" without giving the other person the whole story and your slant on it. There are too many times when a disaster could have been avoided if the person asked had been given more information or someone else's possible solution. If this happens to you, guess who will be blamed?

Assume for these purposes that the other person does not know, or cannot immediately recall, the issues involved. This is always a fair assumption, so you must slither between starting at the very beginning and coming right out with a request for "yes or no." While erring on the side of full disclosure, always keep in mind that it is irritating, and, worse yet, boring to be told all about a matter that has been discussed at every meeting for months. Just keep talking until that glimmer of light shines from across the desk.

## When You Need Them to Say Yes

More important than just getting an answer is getting the right answer—yes. When asking for a favor or information from those who are not beholden to you or who may be strangers, you must first establish some point of contact and empathy. Often these people are government employees or those employed by huge organizations. It is hard for them to see any immediate benefit to helping you. You are in the way!

Here are some suggested approaches.

I am at a loss about this problem and the boss/the client is most insistent. Could you help me . . . ?

I know this is going to be a stretch, but I must have this back by ———. I must warn you that I am often referred to as the East Coast nag distributor.

This is the first time I have ever tried to do this, and I have been told that you know more about it than anyone.

Please have this picked up no later than ———. After that I become destructive.

The more pitiful you sound, the better. Laugh, cry, beg, but never demand or yell unless the person on the other end is depending on your evaluation for a raise or will make some money out of the deal.

If you are skillful and lucky enough to get what you need, please remember your manners. Sincere thank-yous are essential as are notes of appreciation with carbon copies to company presidents, branch managers, supervisors of every kind—the higher the better. Once in a while for very special service, tickets to a local sporting event, books, candy, flowers are appropriate—never cash—unless it is a service for which one usually tips.

Here is an example of a letter of appreciation.

Dear Miss Smith:

Thank you very much for all your help last ——— when I (called/came to) your ——— office to ——— . Your knowledge and patience made an otherwise difficult matter very easy for me. ————company is fortunate, indeed, to have such a responsible and caring person to represent them. Again, many thanks.

Sincerely yours,


cc. Company President
Anyone else you can think of.


The letter can be as long or as short as you like or have time for, but please send it promptly before the matter is forgotten or Jane Smith has moved on to greener pastures.

Notes such as these are an important part of personnel files. You have also given Jane a lift, which she certainly deserves for having treated you so well when you were anticipating surly behavior. You have also given her encouragement to provide similar service to the next person. Who knows, maybe one day everyone will be treated civilly.

Another tip when contacting people for service—avoid asking for favors on Mondays. Many people have a hard time on Mondays and are less apt to respond positively. Try to postpone requests until later in the week. After lunch on Thursday is probably your best bet. You will not get much satisfaction late on Friday unless you are paying the bill. This does not apply to good news, invitations, and compliments, which are most gratefully received on Mondays and any other day of the week.


## When You Need Them to Work with You

Getting cooperation from co-workers, whether they are above or below you on the ladder, is a matter of good sense and manners. It's much like the answer given by the long-married couple when asked how they managed to stay together. "We just try not to annoy each other too much." Even though the quality of the product or service is most important, there is no point in bothering those around you by inappropriate dress, foul language, or insistence on special privileges. Ask for what you need—accept the rest with some degree of grace. Eventually you will get to go home and do what you want.

There are many workplaces where salty language is a sort of dialect, where obscenities appear to make the place homey, where the substitution of "friggin" for "fucking" is deemed an affectation. In other establishments, especially where there are small children and old people who may even claim not to understand, it is important to watch your language. You may be misunderstood and subject the company and yourself to accusations of discrimination or harassment. An occasional obscene word can be very effective as emphasis, but these words should never be used as nouns, verbs, adjectives, and adverbs in every sentence you utter. Frequent obscenity loses its usefulness and resembles more a vocabulary deficiency.

The secret to getting cooperation from others is to cooperate with others. Let it be known that you are willing to share information and knowledge. A very wise man once said to me that there are no secrets in this world. Assume that whatever you have learned from others is general knowledge. The sharing of knowledge is a two-way street. When asked for information or help, do it with a smile, even if not heartfelt. Moans and groans just defeat the whole effect. You may be asking for similar help one day. Sharing information is not the same as doing someone else's job. You should not be expected to do everyone's work. But neither should you reject every request for assistance.

You may have to give a lot to get a little, but you will get something.

There comes a time when letters and telephone calls asking for help do not work. You are reduced to a personal appearance.

Face-to-face communication is becoming increasingly infrequent and therefore more effective. I often get an e-mail from the person in the next office. Sometimes a visit is actually the quickest and most efficient approach of all. It is known as "walking it through."

But it is not as easy as you thought. You have tried to be polite and patiently wait your turn, but nothing is getting done. No one seems to notice you, and if they do, it is only to send you somewhere else to some other person who may be able to handle your request. Fearful that some mysterious extraterrestrial force has rendered you invisible and mute, you take comfort in knowing that you came prepared with pen (not pencil unless it is a recognizably expensive mechanical one) and paper. I use the traditional yellow pad, now more likely to be white, but still clearly something that lawyers use. This marks you as serious, probably a lawyer, and certainly litigious. Another stationery item that gets attention is the steno pad, because it is used by reporters, even more to be feared than lawyers.

When you approach people with pen and pad in hand, they get nervous. Take advantage of this. Write down the date and time and the name of everyone you see. After that you can catch up on your shopping or to-do list. Periodic, obvious notations of the time and discussions with others who also seem to be waiting should get you some attention. Act as if you are interviewing the public and noting down all complaints. I do not suggest that you use this material to get people fired—only to get their attention.

I used this tactic out of pure exasperation when I appeared for the fourth time at the hearing of someone who tried to snatch my purse. The first three times the case was postponed for reasons that I was not told. My pen and pad with lots of movement and conversation with others in the same position got me into the judge's chambers and resulted in some resolution of the matter, not wholly satisfactory, but at least I was spared the inconvenience of returning for the fifth time.

## When You Need Them to Agree with You

It is a great ego deflator to have your brilliant proposal, carefully constructed and in an appropriate cover, torn to shreds by the committee that was supposed to adopt it. What went wrong? You made several mistakes. First, you thought everyone would be grateful that you did all that work yourself and did not bother them. Then, you forgot the important rule about no surprises. And finally, you fell in love with an idea just because it was yours.

If you must work with a group to come up with a single plan or proposal, you can do everything yourself if that is how you choose to work, but be open to the ideas of others and never make an initial presentation of a final copy. That's why we have discussion drafts. It is also a good idea to speak to each member of the group individually during the process just to keep that person on your side. Keep it on a one-to-one basis so that they identify with you and do not gang up against you. Let others have their say and express sincere gratitude for any constructive thought. This is not to say that you must give up on essentials, but very little is accomplished in a democratic society without compromise.

The same principle is applicable to meetings. You may have noticed that when effective people speak in a meeting, they will refer to someone's remarks with approval.

"I quite agree with what John said about the staffing, and I think we should work that idea into our final report."

John beams and is now on your side—whatever it was. Remember to mention as many people as possible. They do not necessarily want to do the work; they just want to make sure that you notice them.

# III
# When to Hold and When to Fold

When you cannot stand the job or the people you work with for another minute, you are facing a difficult decision. When to hold and
when to fold, you ask. What if the next job is worse and all the people are monsters? What if I can't find another job? What will they
say about me? Suppose I have to move and can't sell my house/get
out of my lease? Am I moving around too much?

The decision is easy if:

1. You have just been offered a job in Paris at six times your
   present salary; your spouse is offered the same deal; your
   daughter has just married a French count who insists that you
   stay in his fully furnished apartment overlooking the Seine until you are able to arrange suitable quarters; and you have just
   sold your house for more than the asking price:
   or

2. Your company has just been sold to a competitor and your
   counterpart at the acquiring company is the principal share-
   holder's son-in-law, and your father just decided that you are
   smart enough to run the family business while he retires to
   spend his remaining years studying the Great Frigatebirds and
   Swallow-tailed Gulls in the Galapagos.

If your situation is not close to the above examples, you must
give serious thought to your alternatives. You must consider:

1. What else is available? Do you really have another job or opportunity in hand? I assume that you have already answered advertisements, placed some yourself, and contacted headhunters in your field. Confiding your dissatisfaction to all willing ears will certainly be a problem if you expect to keep at your present employment for any period of time. Remember, there are no secrets, and that as soon as you tell one person, assume that it is general knowledge.

2. What are your resources and responsibilities? Being young with no spouse or children, or maybe living at home with parents who haven't yet turned your room into an art studio, is a great advantage and gives you some breathing space for job hunting.

3. How many jobs have you had during the last five years? A résumé consisting of positions held for six to eighteen months is a sign to prospective employers of a "checkered career." It does not much matter if you left voluntarily or involuntarily. Your application may be discarded in the first cut.

4. Try to judge the situation as accurately as possible. People will rarely tell you the truth about your performance, but you should have some concept of where you stand in relationship to your peers. Try to be realistic. The size of your recent raise or bonus is a fairly reliable barometer. A frank talk with superiors will sometimes provide you with a sense of what is going on. But you will have to plead for an honest evaluation. In these situations truth is hard to come by. When was the last time someone said, "We were thinking of firing you, but we first want to make sure that your replacement is ready to jump right in."

5. Most importantly, do not walk out in a fit of temper just because you are convinced that you are overworked, underpaid, and in general unappreciated. In very short order, your place will be filled and your face forgotten, with nothing accomplished but ill-will and maybe lost opportunities. I remember

very well (I can still feel the pain after twenty-five years) how broken I was when I learned that I had not made partner when I thought it was my due. I dashed off a vituperative letter of resignation, ignoring all the advice given in this chapter. A compassionate young partner wiped my tears, tore up the letter, and gave me words that I shall never forget. "Your success in this life is sometimes measured by just how much shit you can swallow."

6. Above all, keep your own counsel. It will do you no good to moan and groan to co-workers. They cannot help you and will probably make sure your dissatisfaction is known. This gets them the chance to air their gripes without being the bad one.

In times of relatively high employment, people are often lured by what appear to be many choices. It is important to resist, or at least rethink, the urge to switch jobs or abandon whole areas of endeavor because of imagined or even real obstacles. Sometimes waiting it out turns out to be the better course. Let me share with you some of my experiences. When I first started at the law firm, there were places that refused to admit a woman, at least through the front door. And a man and woman not married to each other had to think hard about arrangements when traveling together on business. It was usually suggested that they sleep in different hotels located some distance from each other. In small towns this was a problem.

I recall one particularly galling incident early in my career, about 1963, I think. I was representing a small school district in Pennsylvania that had sold bonds to build a badly needed school house. The closing was to be in New York City. It was usual for the purchaser of the bonds to take everyone out to lunch afterwards. The place selected was the New York Lawyers Club. As we got off the elevator, the host was embarrassed when he was told that women were not permitted in the main dining room, but they would see about getting a private room. Even at the time, I thought it a bit strange since among that group of businessmen, Pennsylvania lawyers, and school district officials, I was the only one licensed to practice law in the State of New York. The one thing I lacked was a penis.

Although I love Philadelphia, it was no better there. I experienced the same barriers and petty annoyances. Sometime in the early 1970s, after I made partner, I tried to join a high-toned Jewish eating club. I was turned down even though I had every requirement, except that all important one. At the time, I was incensed and threatened to sue. The president of the club was a nice man, and at lunch (in the Ladies Dining Room, of course, in the basement) explained that women took too long to eat. I regret to say that I gave up, but I got my revenge some years later when they asked me to join. By that time, the club was less important than I was, so I declined.

When and if you finally decide that you cannot stand it any longer (and you have another offer or very good prospects), resist the temptation to tell everyone off. **LIE.** The following expressions are most appropriate. Another thing I would remind you. You can never lay it on too thick!

I will never forget how much you did for me.
This is a wonderful place to work. I am truly sorry to leave, but the opportunity was just too great.
If I get the chance, I will recommend your product/service.
I would like to keep in touch. May I call you for lunch?
Call me if I can ever do you a favor or you need information I didn't include with the notes I left on my desk.

Since you were one who decided to leave, please be gracious. It will do you no good to leave things in a mess in the vain hope that you will finally get the appreciation you deserve. That will not happen. Your replacement, or those who will have to pick up the slack, will make sure that you get the blame for every error, complaint, or loss of business for the next century. Leave instructions that are as complete as you can make them. It is a nice touch to call back in a few days just to make sure things are working out.

The advice often given about not burning bridges is just as valid if you have been fired. You will probably stay in the same line of work, coming in contact with the same people. It pays to go with some dignity. After all, burning down the place is against the law and you will surely be the prime suspect. You will need a recommendation for the next position. Take some comfort in dreams of a better future. I may be the only person in the world who delights in fantasies of revenge, but I doubt it.

However, you do not have to go like a wimp. Consider your rights under the company's policies. Negotiation may even improve the severance package. No matter what they say, nothing is written in stone and exceptions can be made if you offer sufficient justification. Get everything that is coming to you. Larger establishments have what used to be called the Personnel Department, now known as Human Resources. Those people can be very helpful. Many companies will provide outplacement services or allow you to use the office and routine office services for a while. Take advantage of this. While it may be somewhat depressing for you, it does give you a base of operations, and you do not have to hang around all day. If you need any help that they can provide, just ask. They fired you and should be feeling a little bit guilty. It is important to do all this as soon as you get the word that your services are no longer required. Memories are short in this situation, and you will be forgotten before you know it.

You are certainly entitled to a positive reference letter unless your employer had serious problems with your work or honesty. Your severance pay should continue for the agreed period of time, whether or not you find other employment in that time frame. I always like to include in the release, which is common these days, the employer's agreement to indemnify the employee in case of a suit by a third party for actions done or omitted during the course of employment.

Try to get continuation of your health insurance for a while. After that, you will be able to keep the group health insurance for eighteen months, but you will have to pay for it yourself.

After being fired, most people tend to fantasize about getting revenge. Unfortunately, many forms of revenge are illegal, if not immoral. Better than these illicit fantasies of revenge would be the reality of becoming a great success in your next job or in a profitable business of your own. That'll make them sorry!

To succeed in another position or business, you should, as painful as it may be, try to find out why your services were not considered necessary. Downsizing, mergers, hiring of close relatives of the boss happen. But in too many cases, the trouble is less about your skills and more about the way that you deal with other people.

Make an honest effort to assess your relations with co-workers, customers, clients, and all those other people with whom you have been dealing. It is probably a waste of time to ask them directly, especially those who thought they could get along nicely without you. They will not tell you the truth. They know that you are feeling badly enough, and they definitely do not want any blood on their hands. However, if you are fortunate enough to have a trusted friend or relative with knowledge of your work, that person should be encouraged to be as frank as possible. After that you are on your own. Don't argue, just listen.

# IV
# What Am I Supposed to Do?

In my dreams I imagine a world where one would begin at the top and work down. If you were to work your way down instead of the other way around, you would know just what is expected of you, what the job is meant to accomplish, how you are expected to proceed, and how you are expected to behave while doing it. This is not how it works.

Most of the time, all you have to start with is a job description, if there is one, which doesn't tell you very much. Nor will that advertisement that you answered give you many clues. It told you what a wonderful position awaited you, but little about the actual work. The headhunter who lured you in probably hasn't a clue as to the work involved and is not all that interested. Chances are he or she also neglected to tell you all the disadvantages about the job for fear you would turn it down. It is all on-the-job training. In many cases the people who hired you aren't sure exactly what you will be doing, only the result desired—50 percent increase in net profits.

One of your first and most difficult tasks will be to find out where you fit in and what is expected of you. In some establishments, people are expected to perform only the jobs that they are assigned and in a clearly defined manner. In other places, imagination and creativity are rewarded, and no one cares how you did it just as long as it got done—legally, of course. In most situations people have some degree of freedom to regulate how they work, although not what is to be accomplished. There are enormous variations in any job situation, and experiences from one company to another are typically not transferrable. You were hired and are being paid to perform a certain function, most likely as a part of a series of other functions, so knowing where your part of it fits in is essential.

First try finding out what your predecessor did. Although tempting, try not to change everything all at once until you know why it was done that way. There may have been a good reason for what was done in the past, or maybe it was a good idea then and not now. You will only look foolish if you assume that a seemingly useless activity should be ignored only to discover that without it nothing else worked.

When you work on a matter, project, or assignment, make sure you read everything you can get your hands on. There's gold in them thar hills! Read company brochures, advertisements, annual reports (if it is a public corporation), the history of the business—whatever is not under lock and key or in someone else's desk. A friend of mine once commented that all he knew was what he learned reading upside down. Without being an obvious snoop, you can quickly learn much about the organization.

Get to know the names and faces of all of the higher-ups. They get very upset when someone doesn't acknowledge their exalted position despite the fact they have never, by word or glance, shown any interest in you.

I sincerely believe, and it does no harm to assume, that good work is ultimately rewarded and provides the satisfaction necessary for a good night's sleep. Why not start with that premise rather than assume a them-against-you attitude? The workplace should not be a battleground, but a coordinated effort, which, if successful, will provide something for everyone. It will not do you any good if the company goes out of business. You do not want to be associated with a failure.

The person to whom you report knows, or should know, what the expectations are, but seldom is this information successfully communicated to you. At the very least, the words they use are susceptible to various meanings. People are reluctant to say in clear language what they want you to do and how they expect you to execute the job.

We live in a kind of Tower of Babel in which words are sometimes hard to understand; where the phrase "excuse me" may be an insult; where "I will think about that" means "no"; where "what do you think?" means "you had better agree with me"; where "stay awhile" means "please leave and soon"; and so on.

To be fair, the reason why words can be misleading is because most people want to be liked and do not want to be thought of as overbearing. With this in mind, they resort to vague instructions and soothing euphemisms, which are more likely to lead you astray than guide you down the right path.

For example, how often has someone said to you: "Just get it done at your convenience." This really means that they do not know when they will need it, but it had better be ready the minute they find out.

Here's another one: "I think we should try to organize the sales conference for sometime next year." First of all "we" means you and "sometime next year" means that you should begin immediately to plan the whole thing. Your best attack plan for this situation is to make a list of alternative dates, places, people, etc., and try to make everyone involved concentrate on the particulars of the event so all details get coordinated quickly. If it turns out that every good location is booked by the time you think to inquire about it, the blame will be at your door and your door alone.

Let's do some popular business translations that can catch you off-guard and get you in trouble:

"I wonder where the Jones Report got to." Translation: "You find it."

"Just arrange your vacation whenever it suits the family." Translation: "I have not made my plans yet and have no idea how busy we will be in the next few months." Do not make nonrefundable travel plans. Just pencil in some dates and be prepared to change them.

"I am under orders to cut costs by at least 10 percent, yet maintain productivity and quality." Translation: Uh-oh. This is not a good sign. I suggest that you get yourself on the appropriate committee before they figure out a way to eliminate your job.

"Don't like to trouble you, but sometime could you . . ." Translation: "This is a direct order."

"I was hoping to start reviewing our production schedule sometime." Translation: This is a polite way of telling you to get all your information together quickly and have some good recommendations for improvement.

"Someone really should talk to Joe before he gets himself in a real mess." Translation: "Joe's in trouble and I don't want any of it to rub off on me." Ignore this comment. You do not have enough information about Joe's problems, or the speaker's motives, to get involved.

"There are many fine points in your report, but you might want to refine your ideas and put them in a more cohesive form." Translation: "I have no idea what you are talking about." Start over again.

"We think that you have a great deal of talent that is simply being wasted here." Translation: Start packing. You have been fired, and they do not want to tell you why.

"Everyone does things differently." Translation: This means that either you or your work is out of line, and that you had better get with the program.


In each of these cases, it would be far kinder to tell the person what is expected in plain English, but most people are not like that. In an effort to spare feelings, they conceal and confuse. This is not a kindness. In exasperation I often say, "Just tell me what to do. I'm very obedient." If you are the one who is giving the directives, try to be clear even if you think it might hurt someone. It will hurt even more when misunderstanding leads to finger pointing or lost opportunities.

Then there are the times when you think that you failed to understand and you really haven't. One of the tactics often employed by shrewd businessmen (women find this too inefficient) when negotiating a complex transaction is for each party to state his terms and conditions, smile, shake hands all around, tell the lawyers to draft the documents, and then leave. Of course, no agreement has been reached, but neither has anyone gone off mad. Smart lawyers know what is being done; inexperienced ones think that they are in the Red Queen's Court.

A world of possibilities exists between making sure that you have all the information and permissions necessary to get a job done, and going off half-cocked and faking your way through an assignment. In the nonexistent perfect workplace, all instructions would be written in plain English and never changed. There would also be a kindly, experienced person to answer all questions. It is, and always will be, difficult to know when you should just run with the ball and when you had better check with someone. Many times it just depends on the outcome, which really means that if it turns out all right, you are a hero and if not, you're a you-know-what. The answer is mostly a matter of experience, judgment, and knowing whom you are dealing with at the moment—and luck.

This is one time when others can be very helpful. Anyone who has been on the job for any length of time knows who is the hands-on kind and who just wants to see results. Novices and experts alike are well advised to ask questions and consult with anyone who will give them the time of day. Do not assume that you know everything. Things change constantly, and your work environment is no exception.

When I started doing public finance work, I quickly realized that I didn't even know what I didn't know. This was a bad position to be in. So as not to show my ignorance too often, I would make a list of questions I had, decisions I thought someone else should make, and permissions I needed to go ahead with a project. I would then make an appointment, deceptively saying that I needed only a few minutes, and try to get someone to focus on the deal as a whole. These sessions helped me learn and quieted my frazzled nerves. This method is more likely to get you thoughtful guidance than running in and out of someone's office every time you think of a question. Plus it forces you to focus on the issues rather than your insecurities.

# V
# Getting It Done

Getting others to work with you constructively requires action on your part. They will not do it themselves, sometimes even if you are paying them. So a few words about work discipline.

Few of us are in situations where we start when the bell sounds, move along at a pace mechanically established, and quit when the whistle blows. Equally scarce (good riddance) is piece work, which comes with its own economic motivating force—the faster you work the more you get paid.

Many years ago when I worked as a payroll clerk in a necktie factory in New York, it was my job to count each slip and calculate how much each employee earned for the week. I remember with horror, the stomach-turning pressure on cutters, operators, pressers, and packers to produce, and the heated arguments over each slip.

Thankfully, most of us can exercise some control over our labors either in time or sequence. Some are better at it than others. For those who have joined the work-mostly-at-home set, getting down to work, keeping at it despite distractions, and finishing is a major undertaking, sometimes harder than the work itself. It takes great discipline. I have never been able to work at home except in emergencies. A crisis makes the body produce enough adrenalin to focus the mind and energies without the need for too much additional stimulation.

The number of people who are now working from their homes appears to be increasing, and those who talk about their experiences seem enthusiastic, citing the absence of commuter time and comfortable attire as providing extra time and energy. It may not be a good idea, however, to hang around in your nightclothes. People do come to the door and have been known to peek in windows.

It is probably more difficult to get started and keep at it when no one is around to watch, especially in the home where there are so many distractions. I recall reading about one author who said that he spent hours sharpening pencils and arranging papers, putting off the actual act of writing for long periods of time. For those working on a word processor, it is possible to waste hours with computer games, which do not even give you a chance at a big hit like the slots. I tell you this so that you know you are not alone.

There are some tricks of the trade, however, that can help.

Lists are a valuable tool. The very act of writing things down has some organizational merit. Assigning degrees of importance and time spans (even if not strictly adhered to) provides a sense of control over one's life. Any kind of list will do, as long as it is on a single sheet of paper and kept right in front of you. If you need a second page, either you have too much to do or have done too little about it. Some people use those notes that stick to the telephone, desk, computer, or refrigerator. These may have been the greatest boon to efficiency in this century, but, like contraceptive methods, they don't work if you don't use them.

The clock is also a handy vehicle. Make the clock a toy—play with it, talk to it, make promises to it, tell it to go slower, go faster. Use time as a spur and a reward to yourself. I will read so many pages, write so many letters, add so many columns, make so many calls each twenty minutes. One hour of (a disagreeable task) and then I can (agreeable task). The faster you work, the faster time will pass. This is my own version of the law of relativity.

Clean desk or piles of paper? I cannot help you here. Years of observation have demonstrated that there are efficient people of both persuasions and all sorts between. A clean desk sometimes looks unproductive, posing the ever-present danger of forgetting the matter. If you keep everything on your desk until it is finished, try not to confuse Mr. Smith's order for a bridal bouquet with Mr. Jones's order for a funeral wreath.

Stiff folders with easy-to-read labels are good friends. I like the kind that are closed on three sides and expand. However, be careful what you put in those folders. Look at the label carefully. Never shove a handful of paper in unless you are sure everything belongs there. Once in the wrong folder, forever in the wrong folder and lost for good.

Ideally one should pick up a project and keep at it until it is completed. But life doesn't work that way. Rarely will all those other people have done their part and given it to you on time and in proper order. But if you heed my words, it will happen more and more. It is probably not worthwhile waiting for everything to come together before starting. But you will just get everyone mad if you hand in your part before they have put their two cents in. See chapter VIII—Nagging.

What is important is having the basics in place with enough comprehensible notes to tell you what you are missing, who is going to supply it, and when it must be done. What is most essential (here's where those folders come in) is keeping all this information in one place.

Having many things to do is one way of getting a lot done. The old saying about giving a job to a busy person to make sure it gets done is still true. Maybe a secretary or assistant wound up with the task, but no matter. We are only interested in results. The less time you have, the more efficient you become, simply because there is no alternative.

Women who manage a home and children while holding down a full-time job or others burdened with two full-time jobs learn to make the most of each and every minute. For most, the day is longer, but it is vital that the time spent on each activity be productive. These people have learned to:

31

1. Keep telephone conversations to a minimum. After the information has been communicated, get off the phone as quickly as good manners permit. We all hate answering machines and voice mail, but it does discourage idle chatter, reduces the number of those pink slips, and in many cases can move a project forward with each call.

2. Use catalogues for buying things that do not need to be tried on or carefully inspected. Catalogues are an industry that has changed the buying habits of millions in one generation. My own experience shows these companies to be both responsive and responsible. The sheer number of available catalogues is somewhat daunting, but I must assume that it is worth the costs of printing and postage. An industry that has changed the shopping habits of so many in so short a time must know what it is doing, but duplicate, and ofttimes, triplicate copies of the same expensive brochure make me wonder.

3. Make a list at the end of the day of those things that were not done. This really serves a dual purpose. You are better organized in the morning and feel smug when leaving.

4. Eat lunch with someone, an associate, customer, competitor, or boss, if you can. You never know what information you can pick up. You are just wasting your time if you eat at a counter with your nose in the newspaper.

5. Try to start right away. Avoid delays unless absolutely necessary. If your alimentary system requires certain activities to be done at 9:00 A.M., it cannot be helped. We are not robots. We are all human beings, after all. We must make allowances.

6. Keep several things going at one time. Having only one thing to do leads to gross inefficiencies—and boredom.

7. Try to use both hands to do two things at the same time. I had an aunt who was able to wash dishes with one hand and keep a cigarette burning in the other. I do not recommend this par-

ticular activity, but I use it to illustrate what can be done with a little imagination.

Having too little to do is deadly. I remember my first, real full-time job. I was hired (I have forgotten how this came to be) as assistant secretary to Judge Dorothy Kenyon. She was not on the bench at that time, and she shared office space with another woman lawyer in a building at 50 Broadway in New York City. Since she had a very good secretary, who had been with her for many years, there was very little for me to do. The days were long and I had a hard time keeping awake. Each day I hoped that my in-box would fill up, but because there wasn't much to do, and as I lacked typing and shorthand skills, the pickings in the in-box remained slim.

Time just dragged, and I realized that I was not even worth the pittance I received each week. It was time to move on. It is a mistake to stay in a situation where you know you are not needed. You should either expand your duties or find other employment. This is an addition to the rules of chapter III—"When to Hold and When to Fold," but the same principles apply.

There are a great many people who would rather surprise others than disappoint them. They are prone to underestimate their skills so that when the work is produced, it will be a delightful surprise and enhance their reputations. They tend to start every job with cautionary statements like:

I really have no experience with this.
I never did this before.
I'm not sure I can do this.

Statements like these are more apt to get you passed over in favor of an individual with more willingness to try. You do not have to advertise your deficiencies; people will find out soon enough. In the meantime, this may be a good chance to learn something new. No one is asking you to build a space ship. Naturally, you would not lie about your experience, but you cannot tell what you can do until you have tried. You might try substituting the following for the three negative statements above:

I have not done this exact type of ——, but I have a good idea
    from other —— I have done in the past.
This should be interesting.
I may need a little extra time, but it is certainly doable.

What you are attempting to do is to build confidence, not incredulity. What you are doing to yourself is stretching your knowledge and abilities. And that is what you need to do to get ahead and to gain greater satisfaction from your job as well as the respect of others. Respect is important if you want others to work with you and not against you.

A cautionary word about telling the truth. What you do with your friends, family, and lovers is your own business, but lying in a work situation is dangerous and plays havoc with your stomach lining. Many people believe that lying is just not telling the truth when asked a direct question. Lying is also holding back important information that might have been elicited if the right questions were asked. Be careful how you interpret a question. Even when not under oath, others get very upset when they discover that they have been made to look foolish. In the work situation, the truth is vital. You should just temper it with enthusiasm and willingness to try new things.

# VI

# Mistakes

## Your Mistakes

You will make mistakes—lots of them. The trick is to make less of them than the other fellow. There is no use denying to yourself (later about denying to others) that you have made an error. It is done. Just try to avoid making the same one again.

A mistake, regardless of the consequences, is also no reason to retreat from the arena. Risk is something we all must take if we are to succeed in any endeavor. To avoid ever making a mistake, one would have to work at the most menial job, never aspire to anything, live in a cocoon, have nothing to do with the opposite sex, certainly never marry or have children, or do anything fun, interesting, or potentially profitable.

Mistakes are inevitable and frequent; the issue is what to do when they happen.

My mother taught me a valuable lesson one day when I came home with a disastrous haircut. She saw me weeping bitterly and tugging in vain to encourage faster growth. She said, "You don't have to wear your mistakes or live with them. What you have to do is to pay for them." In this context, paying means more than just money. It would be easy if all we had to do is to throw money at our mistakes to make them disappear. Fixing means making amends, remedying the situation, containing the damage, and probably paying out some bucks as well.

Confession may be good for the soul, but it is bad for the career. Divulge mistakes on a strict need-to-know-basis. Tell only those whose help you absolutely require, or those who might also be held accountable for the error. All others will commiserate but secretly gloat. There is nothing like hearing about the misfortunes of others to make us feel better about our own shortcomings.

It has been suggested that the urge to confess mistakes is gender related, women being more prone to advertise their mistakes than men.[2] I think it is also related to inexperience and the unfortunate fact that women are less likely to have some experienced person to show them the ropes and the folly of belittling oneself. Leave that to others. It makes them feel good.

Whether it was your mistake or just something you could have prevented does not alter the situation. Start the process of fixing, again, without making a major production out of it.

But before you do anything, please remember:

1. you are not doing brain surgery;[3]
2. the world is not coming to an end;
3. memories are very short;
4. embarrassment is not fatal.

If it is any comfort, you try thinking of yourself as a dot on what Stephen Hawking calls a minor planet going around a very average star in the outer edge of a typical galaxy that is only one of a hundred billion galaxies we can see.

If the whole world finds out about the problem before you are able to contain the damage, it is important to resist the temptation to lie, offer an alibi, or blame someone else. Go off for a while to collect your thoughts, get the facts, and plan out the remedy. Don't

2. Mendell, Adrienne, *How Men Think* (New York: Ballantine Books, 1996).
3. If you are engaged in brain surgery or a similar line of work, please skip the rest of this chapter.

take too much time at this stage. All you really want to do is show others that you have the situation in hand.

Do not spend a great deal of time explaining how it happened, what you were thinking at the time, why it could not have been avoided. None of this is relevant and nobody cares. This is true even though the first questions you will get are: "How could you?" "What were you thinking of?" "Couldn't you have ———?" It is the past. Ignore these questions if possible. Otherwise keep your answer short and vague. Something like:

I thought it best at the time, or
I know now that it was the wrong thing to do, or
I really should have investigated further.

Do not prolong this part of the conversation. Start immediately with damage control and repair.

This is the time, however, to consult with others who have a stake in the matter and may even have faced the situation themselves. Go as far up the ladder as you safely can. Those beneath you are even less likely to know what to do and may be less inclined to help. Also resist the temptation to dump it on someone else, unless some Good Samaritan with experience in the matter offers to assist.

Even if you are fortunate enough to have a noble friend who offers to fix everything for you while you recover your equilibrium, it is not a good idea to go off and let others take care of the matter. First of all they do not know everything about the situation, and, more importantly, you want to have some say in how your actions are being portrayed. People are less likely to paint you as a total idiot when you are in the same room with them. I know it is painful, but stay the course.

Sometimes you get very lucky and the worst mistake you ever made in your whole life turns out to be a spectacular success. Brains, experience, hard work are all very important, but you just can't beat luck. Once, through inexperience and plain ignorance, I agreed to do something that no one else had ever done before for the very good reason that it was prohibited in the relevant documents. Fortunately, other smarter people were then forced to review the situation and come up with a way to do it. Eventually, the procedure became accepted and I got the credit for being the first to do it. It is both a comfort and a recognition of one's limitations to remember that much of what happens is a matter of luck.

It sometimes happens the other way round. The thing that you did perfectly well turns out bad. Life is like that. You have control over only a part of what is happening. We may be the captains of our fate and masters of our souls, but others have important supporting roles in our lives as well. We did not pick our parents or great-grandparents, and we certainly did not pick our bodies, although here is something we can work on.

You will probably survive your mistakes, but you will not be able to avoid making all of them. Of course you will make them, but unless you are involved in serious illegal operations, prison time is highly unlikely.

## Mistakes of Others

Since we all know that but for the grace of God we could be in the same spot, gloating is not permitted, nor is advertising the misfortunes of others, even if it occurred through pure stupidity. Just be thankful that this time you got away.

On the other hand (nothing is ever simple), there are times when you will find yourself in a spot where you know something is wrong, the perpetrator is not owning up, and great harm might result. These situations are tough, but err on the side of discretion and do not rush in with accusations unless you are sure and have some solid evidence. These are among the toughest calls and involve too many possibilities for this small book. After a great deal of thought and consultation with people you trust, you may decide that you could not live with yourself if you do not speak up. Good luck!

It is difficult enough to learn from your own blunders and it is probably impossible to learn from the errors of other people. Having said all this, you may want to keep in mind what has happened in the past and what has worked or not worked.

I have learned from bitter personal experience (my mother told me but I did not listen to her) not to fight other people's battles. I think it important to keep a balance between wanting to be helpful to co-workers and getting so deeply involved that the outcome becomes your responsibility, and any harm done becomes your fault while the true malefactor has somehow squirmed out of it.

Be as helpful as you can within the limits of your time and experience. If you know the solution because it either happened before or you are sure you know the true course, by all means be a friend. But do not neglect your job and family just because it is easier to deal with the problems of others than to face your own work and responsibilities. Be as good to yourself as you are to others—better.

There is an old Yiddish saying: "A man who is too good to others is not good for his family."

# VII
# Working with Very Difficult People

In some other world, there is a place where all work is precisely organized, carefully planned to fit the talents and knowledge of those assigned the tasks, and always completed just in time to be used, no earlier, no later. Everyone who works there is also organized, experienced, and always on time with each part of the job. This place is called Eden. But ever since Adam and Eve bit into that apple, nobody has been able to find it.

Everywhere else, people who always do an exemplary job in the allotted time are not so easy to find. Most work is done reasonably well and within certain flexible time constraints by conscientious people with a fair understanding of what they are doing. For the most part, these people should be supervised but not too closely, corrected when necessary, and encouraged by some form of recognition. Money qualifies for this purpose, but words of praise are close behind.

There are, however, several specific types who clog up the works and drive us absolutely crazy.

In no particular order of difficulty, they are:

1. PROCRASTINATORS. Those people who put things off until the very last moment. They claim that they can only work under pressure or throbbing with the hot glow of creation. The truth is that they are easily distracted. They seem not to recognize that the rest of us are under pressure to get the work out. We would also like to be able to organize our day so that we can get home at a reasonable hour. High on this list of malfeasors are the people who

give secretaries work just after 4:45 P.M. and insist that it get out that day even though all possible recipients have gone off on a three-week holiday.

So far no one has discovered a procrastination gene. No one is predestined to be late for everything. And the old maxim about it being well worth the wait rarely applies to the end product put out by a procrastinator.

The good news is that, of all the difficult people you will work with, the procrastinator is the most easily retrained.

Procrastination is eminently treatable. All you have to do is not put up with it. The procrastinator responds very well to firm, explicit directions.

If it isn't on my desk by noon, I will get Joe to do it.
If you're not at the table by 7:25 P.M., eat somewhere else.
If you haven't finished it by 5:00 P.M., just leave what you have and I will finish it myself.
I am telling you right now that I will not wait for you one minute after 1:15 P.M.

The point is to follow through. It may be somewhat inconvenient the first time, but the procrastinator is not obstinate and learns fast. The procrastinator knows who will, and who will not, put up with delay. You just be the one who won't.

If you are the procrastinator and are unwilling to change, you should work and live alone. If this does not appeal to you, or it is too late to change careers and jettison your family, I suggest that you change your ways and pay more attention to the clock. This takes some discipline and a modification of your usual mode of behavior, but you really can do it. There are all sorts of behavior-modification methods, but all of them start with you. You must want to change and then you must do something about it.

2. BIG PICTURE PEOPLE. They get the ideas and then leave it to others to carry them out. If you can get away with this

type of behavior, then you are the boss and do not need any advice from me.

Big picture people tend to forget the basic rules of management. "Organize, delegate, and supervise." To this I might add that it helps if you have done it yourself before. The result of ignoring that basic rule is chaos. Ideas are wonderful. Chapter XII—"More Worlds to Conquer," is full of them, but these things do not get done by themselves. Execution, marketing, and, in many cases access to capital, is needed.

Big picture people move around a lot, so you are sure to encounter one during your career. If you are working for a big picture person, be prepared for change and confusion. Big picture people are sometimes exciting to work with, but they will waste your time and can be expensive.

If you are the big picture person, my advice is to hire someone else to follow through and pay that person very well.

3. I'M DONE. These are the people who do a down and dirty job and then go off without a second glance. It is like the advice given during the war in Vietnam: "Just say we've won and leave."

This sort of person should only be given the kind of work that cannot possibly be finished before it is done right. Like flagpole-sitting or lion-taming. If you must work with one of these types, be sure to check everything. They may not like it and may even get nasty, but you have an interest in a job well done. At the first opportunity, after making darn sure that you will not be blamed, let the work go out without correction. Either you have been too fussy or they are too sloppy. At least you will find out.

4. PERFECTIONISTS. I love these wonderful worriers who seem to carry the weight of the world on their shoulders and seek perfection with blithe ignorance of the fact that it is out of human reach. They are frustrating, expensive, and make you feel as if you are an idiot. It may be some comfort to know that they are not any easier on themselves.

These are the people who cannot understand that not everything requires the same degree of care, and few people are in a position or willing to pay for the time that it takes to achieve perfection. This is a goal best left for the next world.

Perfectionists simply cannot understand that very few lives are defined by a single act; that changes are inevitable, mostly because people keep changing their minds; that others will gladly accept and pay good money for what is merely well done; and that time really is money.

On the other hand, while those who find it hard (if not impossible) to let go of a piece of work can make you tear your hair out, they can also make you successful and rich if you learn how to deal with them.

How to work with a perfectionist:

1. Perfectionists like to work on one thing at a time. Do not permit this or the work will never get done.
2. They need constant assurance of the value of their work (and your love) because they are insecure and keep imagining all sorts of catastrophes if everything isn't perfect.
3. Be very patient. Nagging in this case is counterproductive because by now they have built up a lifetime immunity.
4. Give work in stages rather than all at once. Perfectionists have trouble putting things in perspective.
5. Perfectionists like to work alone. Do not permit this. Left to their own devices, the perfectionist is capable of offering further suggestions to a customer who has finally agreed to purchase, at full retail price, the item that you thought you would never unload.
6. Put limits on time and cost, but allow some leeway. Words like budget, schedule, deadline, competitor, are simply not in their vocabularies.

If you are the perfectionist, please understand how difficult you are to work with and have some pity on the rest of us mortals.

Also remember that you were asked to do a job for one of two reasons; either someone thought enough of your abilities to ask for you or else you were the only one around. While it is essential to do the job right, it is just as important to get it done. The most damaging thing that could happen to you is to work so long on a project that it is no longer needed, or worse, was completed by someone else who won an award.

Through your contacts with perfectionists, you will learn one thing: patience. You may also learn that when a thing is done well, it is truly a joy—provided it somehow gets finished.

# VIII
# Nagging

Nagging has an unfortunate reputation, derived largely from comedians who use the words "wife" or "mother-in-law" as a substitute for humor. In the world of work, nagging is both useful and most effective when used properly, not too often, and for good and sufficient reasons. Knowing when to nag is essential when faced with people who do not always have your best interests at heart, and, understandably, think mostly of their own. Knowing how to nag is an art form, requiring the delivery and timing skills of a borscht circuit comedian.

Nagging is a stand-alone method, which should not be accompanied by any other technique for getting others to work with you. Particularly dangerous is the use of ridicule and sarcasm. Too many people cannot resist the temptation to make fun of others, thinking that such remarks count as great wit and taking offense is a sign of a poor sport. Ridicule defeats any chance of a successful nag and can win you a longtime enemy. They may laugh now, but plan revenge tomorrow, or as soon as an opportunity presents itself—when you are down.

Ridiculing others when they are out of earshot is almost as bad as when they are present. They will be just as angry, but later, when word gets back.

We may not realize it, but many occupations are basically nagging—getting others to do their work—properly and on time. I would rather not resort to a euphemism. It is what it is—NAGGING.

# Nagging Yourself

You actually nag yourself all the time. You nag yourself with reminders, alarm clocks, and all sorts of tugs on your time and memory. This helps eliminate some of the nagging required from others. However, reminders cannot do their job if you have left out important information. Your reminders should contain all the information you need. It is no help to have a note that says "Lunch 12:30" unless it also tells you with whom and where. Discipline yourself to write down as much information as you will need. By the time the day arrives, you will probably have forgotten many of the details. I find those tiny engagement books to be a menace and prefer those that do not try to get the whole week on one three-by-five sheet of paper.

These days many people use their computers as engagement books, but unless you carry it around with you, I can't see the benefit. For electronics addicts, there are some interesting new products on the market, which are small enough to be portable and can be used to note down appointments as well as names, addresses, and telephone numbers that you want to keep.

# Nagging Others

Nagging others should be done gently, with some offer of assistance where practicable. Try to precede your verbal nag with an offer to do something to get the work started, and keep your tone calm and somewhat matter of fact, as if you do it to everyone all the time. Written nagging is most effective when it contains an outline or enough information to get started. Nagging should have a purpose, a goal. To reach that goal, a person needs to nag correctly and to follow the ten nagging rules:

1. Nagging is a repetitive process. To tell someone something

only once is not nagging. It is usually thought of as a suggestion.

2. Nagging loses its effectiveness when employed for trivial matters.

3. It is rude to nag in front of others. We want people to be motivated, not embarrassed.

4. Identify the people (there aren't a lot of them) who never need nagging and get pretty huffy about being reminded of something that they said they would do.

5. No screaming.

6. Being known as one who is persistent (a nag) is not all that bad. It may mean that people pay more attention to your requests.

7. Never nag when you are angry. The purpose of nagging is to get something done that you cannot do by yourself. Provoking an argument will not accomplish the deed.

8. Smile. If appropriate, accompany the verbal nag with a compliment or some innocuous preface like: "I know how busy you have been lately, but—."

9. Nagging is not the method of last resort; the whip is. Nagging is useful only if employed before you have run out of patience, all deadlines have been missed, or you are out of a job.

10. No poking or other physical contact.

## The Naggee

If you are the naggee, don't be insulted. Take it as a compliment. Apparently, you are the only person who can do the particular job. If they could find someone else, they would have nagged someone else rather than bother you.

# IX

# How to Find Practically Everything

No matter how smart you are, your brain cannot hold all the information amassed over time—and who would want to anyway when there are all those other brains just pulsating with knowledge and eager to impart it.

But before you bother all those other people, you should try to get as much information as you can by yourself. Doing what you can first will give you enough information to narrow the field and avoid the appearance of utter stupidity.

## The Internet

The Internet has changed the information business—completely, forever, and for the better. If you have access at home or at work, the Internet and the World Wide Web should be your first stop when trying to research a company, a stock, medical advances, your heritage, your child's homework—and almost anything else you can think of.

But be prepared and do not be in a rush. By typing in a few keywords, you are likely to find hundreds, if not thousands or tens of thousands of listings that claim to have just what you're looking for. The truth is, however, that many of the sites will be irrelevant, offering a weak link to the subject that you entered, and a few may be pornographic. (Don't take that personally.)

If you are lucky, you will find just what you are looking for the first time around and you can download the information to your disk, print it out, and go on with your life. Most of the time, you will have to dig a bit deeper and refine your search. Don't worry, it will be worth the effort, and you will get better at it as you go along. If you have trouble, ask a nearby child.

I have found that the Web is the perfect place to start a research project and a quick look at Web sites will let you know who the experts are (or those who think they are) in almost any field, from the most mundane to the most esoteric. But despite the vast quantities of information on the Web, it may not have what you want. So, if this happens, use the Web as a telephone directory to help you find sources of additional information One of the best examples of this is the federal government Web sites. All departments have a site and, in addition to the information they think you want, provide contact information that will lead you to what you really need.


## Your Tax Dollars at Work

Despite what you may have heard, my experience with the federal bureaucracy has, for the most part, been most positive. Generally, these people are willing and able to help find the information you need. The key, as you might imagine, is patience. Within the Department of Commerce alone, there are hundreds of people, each of whom is in charge of a very specific area like South American coffee, or Caribbean mangos. The point is that someone, somewhere, knows what you want to find out.

Just ask. And ask. And ask again. Because it will most likely take you three, four, five or more contacts before you get the right person. And then they might not be at their desk. But guess what? They do return phone calls. The best part is that all the information, and there is an amazing amount of it, is free. Just for the asking.

Your representative to Congress has a staff and part of their job is to keep you happy, for which they hope you will be grateful on election day. They may not be able to solve the problem, but they can get you a name to ask for or the name of the department or agency that handles the matter. If the name, address, telephone number, and fax number of your congressperson or senator suddenly escapes you, this information can sometimes be found in the Blue Pages in your local phone directory. You can also get it by calling your local library or office of the League of Women Voters.

What the federal government doesn't know is what the states are doing and so your next stop might be your state or municipal government. Here again, your first stop should be the office of your representative. In my experience, getting information from state and local officials can be a bit trickier than on the federal level. I don't know why, but state and local employees, as a rule, do not seem to be as anxious to help a faceless voice on the other end of the telephone. That is why it is so important to be able to say that "Councilman/Assemblyman/Representative ———— thought that you might be able to help me with this problem."

## Your Library

Just for fun, take a trip to your local library. If you have not spent much time there recently, you may be shocked at the amount of information it contains—everything from original historical documents to the latest and greatest in computer information access. Did you know, for example, that thousands of pages of government research is available on the Web, and that all you have to do is to bring a diskette to your library and download what you need?

Your library has directories and source materials that, if they do not contain the answer to your question, will certainly help point you in the right direction. For example, the *Encyclopedia of Associations* lists thousands of associations. Some are in the business arena, others in the arts and science. If there is a reason for more than one person to care about something, there is an association for it. Call them. They are often eager to help you get what you need.

The library also has computer access (forget the microfilm unless you are going way back) to magazine files. You can search by subject, author, keyword, etc. When you find an article you want, most libraries have printers attached that will allow you to print the information that you need at a nominal charge per sheet. Alternatively, bring your diskette and download the information.

When you are doing research, any type of research, make your reference librarian your best friend. Make a donation and mention their name. Volunteer. Send a notice to the supervisor, board of trustees, mayor and/or anyone else with authority. Mention them in the credits. Everyone likes to see their name in print. That is why books have pages of acknowledgment and acceptance speeches are so long. Letters to the editor are a great way to call special attention to someone's efforts on your behalf.

Do whatever you have to do to get the librarian on your side. These people went to school for years to learn how to find information. Many of them are quite good at it. Those who aren't can make up for a lack of experience with effort—if they want to and you stand there long enough. It is their job and, like most of us, they really do want to do it well and receive appropriate acknowledgment for their efforts.

If you are serious about research, take an afternoon just to browse the reference section of your library. If the reference librarian is available, ask for a quick tour. It will serve you well and you will have made a contact and maybe a friend. Remember to get the librarian's name. Write it down so that you can ask for him or her by name the next time.

# E-mail

E-mail is a wonderful way to ask for information from many people with a stroke of the key. The great thing about it is the ease of replying, which means that you are more likely to get what you need. In larger organizations you have the advantage of being able to direct your request to whole departments, or the whole company! Literally hundreds of potential sources with a click of a button. It is truly amazing! Just a quick cautionary note about e-mail, however. Once it's sent, it's gone—like mailing a letter in a corner mailbox. If you choose the wrong group, you're past the point of no return. And, if there is anything the least bit personal, remember that e-mail does not get deleted right away—even with the delete key. This is in part how many people get into trouble. But assuming nothing you have written would embarrass you on the front page of your local paper, just go ahead.

Recently I was asked by an old friend about a company that contacted her about lost assets of a relative who had died over twenty years ago. It sounded like a scam. I used my e-mail to request information from about six hundred people. Within fifteen minutes I had responses from three people whom I had never met. One had previously worked for the company and vouched for its legitimacy. The second knew the person who had contacted my friend. And the third explained how similar businesses worked and told me that it was worthwhile pursuing. The result was several thousand dollars of found money.

## There's So Much More . . .

Let your fingers do the walking—while geographically limited, the category breakdown in the Yellow Pages is simply amazing. Often you can look up one category and be led to two or three other related subjects that you had not even considered.

It has been said that each of us is separated from all others by, at most, six degrees of separation. This means that someone you know knows someone who knows what you need to know. Got that? The point is that most people are happy to help and show how smart they are, or to refer you to someone who can. The others simply do not count.

If there is a reason for more than one person to care about something, there is an association for it. Get the number from an association directory and call. They are often eager to help you get what you need as long as you are not out to destroy their business or start a lawsuit.

Like associations, there is a magazine for just about anything you can think of. You can find them all listed in a number of sources, such as *Bacon's Media Directory*. This volume will list all the magazines that address specific areas, such as the cosmetic industry, or banking, or whatever. Call the appropriate magazine (they list names and telephone numbers), ask for the editorial department (not advertising or circulation), and explain your dilemma. Typically they are happy to help, sometimes for free and sometimes just for the cost of a back issue. Newspapers, especially dailies with overworked editors on constant deadlines, are typically not as helpful; however, many are offering research services of their own. Or, try checking with reporters who cover the area in which you are interested.

For business-related information, try calling the public relations departments of companies in the field.

Fortunately, to date, I have yet to find a question that I can't answer given enough time and patience. It's positively amazing the things that people know.

# X

# Combining Your Efforts with Theirs[4]

Nothing will fall off if a man reads this chapter, but its message will have more relevance for today's women who are struggling to combine the traditional homemaker role with full-time employment.

Plato, a liberal among the early philosophers, thought that women could be just as reasonable as men if they were trained in the same way as men and, of course, were relieved of all child-rearing and household duties.

John Stuart Mill, also given high marks among the philosophers for his enlightened views of women, assumed that all women had many servants, and that an hour a day was more than enough to take care of household matters. After that they could spend the rest of their days in study and contemplation.

In a simpler time, women, and the few men who supported equality of the sexes, really believed that the elimination of legal impediments, the right to vote, and equal access to all fields of endeavor, would provide women with the good life and free them from total dependence on fathers and husbands. The arguments against spoke of women's physical delicacy, emotional sensitivity, weakness of intellect, and need for special protection. Nowhere was it argued that she might be worse off because she would be burdened with two full-time jobs. But that is precisely what

4. This chapter is an expansion of an article which appeared in *The Philadelphia Lawyer,* Winter 1997.

happened for most women. Now instead of being slave to one master, she has found herself slave to many.

In my generation women who aspired to professional careers planned to alternate career with home responsibilities. The plan was to finish your education, marry, work for two years, have two children, stay home until the second child entered whatever institution that kept him or her for most of the day, and then return to your career exactly where you left off, or maybe, just a few months behind everyone else. I don't think that we ever considered colds, vacations, teacher's conferences, and certainly not out-of-town travel. We probably assumed that someone's mother would just fill in. We must also have assumed that the situation that we returned to would be exactly the same as when we left. All the same people, no new inventions, procedures, or laws, the same customers and clients and more importantly, the same governmental forces at work.

What was wrong with that plan? Everything! To begin with, everyone's mother either had a job herself or lived in Florida. Then there were all those days when school was not in session or children were sick. On top of that, if you wanted to get ahead, or even keep your job, the hours could become erratic.

I can also tell you from my own experience that if you leave your job for any extended period, when you return (provided they let you return), you will find yourself at the bottom of the pack. Everything has changed. Your friends are gone, and all those new people are giving you the fish eye. There is a completely new software system in place, which everyone says is terrific, but it looks like Greek to you. The new CEO looks about twelve years old. You must buy a whole new wardrobe before you even start to work. And, in many professions, you will be required to make up years of continuing education credits.

Women should not be forced into an all-or-nothing choice. Neither they nor the economy can afford it. There are many positions that have always been part-time or where hours are more or less flexible. (I do not refer to shift work because two parents working different shifts seems to be the least desirable solution. Besides, a woman will still find herself doing two full-time jobs.) Part-time work is a practical solution for some, and it is the norm in many occupations.

Working from home with all the new communication methods is also a viable option, but care must be taken to return to the workplace so that others do not forget you. Human beings are still social animals and you are less likely to be ignored or forgotten if you show up on a regular basis. And, while you are there, make sure that everyone sees you. Do not sneak in and out again. They will think you don't like them, and they will return the compliment. There is also the danger that you will be viewed as non-essential, therefore, the first in line to be let go if downsizing occurs.

For some, the solution is simply to start your own business and control your own life. That road is beyond the scope of this book. You will find a wealth of other material on the subject. Many women have made a successful transition to entrepreneurship, and I salute them. They know how to work and do not need me.

In those pursuits that usually call for extended education and extended hours, accompanied by larger pay checks and more prestige, the opportunities for flexible work weeks are tragically limited. It is here that women must forge their own way and employers must facilitate the process. Not to do so is to lose competitive edge.

Unless new systems are put in place, companies will find that they have spent a great deal of time and money training young women only to have them leave just when the training is beginning to pay off. More often what starts out as a sabbatical turns into unintended retirement. These highly educated and trained young women are forced to find less demanding activities or abandon their careers entirely, and this is not an efficient system. A way must be found to permit women to continue their careers through the years when family responsibilities are heavy and when many women wish to maintain close contact with their growing children.

There is a way, and I hope that more women would use it so that their lives can be varied without being harried. And as an extra benefit, their productiveness will add to the economy.[5]

Two people (either men or women or one of each) who wish to remain active in the work force yet reduce the amount of time devoted to it (for whatever reason) can form a kind of partnership.[6] Some may call this job sharing, but it is much more. It is a cooperative arrangement between two people whereby the combined efforts reduce the efforts required by each. These combined efforts will result in more brainpower and energy available for the work involved.

This partnership will consist of people who function as a single interchangeable unit with a common goal, that goal being the delivery of a product or service with no breaks in the process. It assumes that the partners share similar goals, are prepared to share the rewards and responsibilities, and are determined to compete with the outside world rather than with each other.

This is not a new concept, only its application. The people involved must be flexible. The prospective partners need not be best friends or even wish to maintain social contact, but they should know each other's work habits. Someone who cannot rest unless everything is done in advance simply would not be able to tolerate someone who cannot do a thing until the very last minute. Thus, they should have some experience working together so they can identify possible snags and any areas of conflict. A trial period is

5. You are either producing or aiding the production.
6. If the number is greater than two, the scheme becomes more complex in terms of communication and management. This group should work as a closed unit without additional services or devices.

probably not feasible because both parties will have made provision for the change from full to part-time employment, including less money.

When considering this kind of arrangement, the two parties need to discuss and settle several issues, among them:

1. The division of time. Who will be in the workplace and when? This division will probably form the basis of the monetary split, but not necessarily, for example in the case where one partner brings more to the table than the other in terms of experience or business. If the remuneration each receives is not based on hours, then periodic adjustments should be considered.

2. Is the arrangement for a specific time period, or project, or is it an "at will" arrangement, which means, until one of the parties wishes to withdraw? Many parents find that as their children grow older, it is more important than ever for them to be close at hand. Supervision, guidance, and example replace the purely physical care required by small children. This partnership arrangement can take on a continuing life of its own for an unlimited period of time, with or without the original participants.

3. What happens in the event of an emergency, either at the workplace or in the home? Both of the partners should be able to contact the other at all times. This means not only home telephone numbers, but car phones, beepers, or cellular phones. As time goes by, there should be less need for frequent communication.

4. I suggest setting a regular time each week to meet and go over pending work. This is the time when the benefit of using two heads and the experience of two people will come into play. Suggestions and possible corrections should be encouraged by each of the partners, because the quantity and quality of the finished product benefits both.

5. This is a business arrangement. It would seem best to avoid a close personal relationship and certainly one that involves others, such as spouses or children. We do not need any more areas of possible conflict to contend with—clients, customers, bosses, and government agents are enough.[7]

6. People's work habits are varied, especially when it come to how cluttered or neat they keep their work space. You are not likely to find a partner who is exactly like you in this respect, so some compromise is in order. Ideally, each of the partners will have a separate workspace, office, desk, or area. If space must be shared, there should be serious discussions about its condition. Posters of unclad persons are not to everyone's taste.

7. Disagreements must be settled by the partners themselves. It defeats the whole purpose of the arrangement if an outsider is brought in to negotiate partnership matters.

8. How you will present yourselves? The object here is to achieve a oneness in the eyes of the people with whom you work. The use of "we" instead of "I" is the place to start. For example: "We thought that . . ." or "Call us when . . ." or "What do you want us to do . . ." and "How shall we contact you?"

9. It must be clear to both partners that any mistakes are the mistakes of both, as are the honors achieved.

I suspect that finding your partner will be more difficult than getting the organization to accept the proposal. But let us never underestimate organizational resistance to change. The usual objections will be raised:

"It will cost more." Answer: Cost is just a number. We can di-

---

7. This is disputed by two very successful lawyers who have been job sharing for over eight years. They are personal friends and their families often share holiday meals.

vide most of the benefits, and besides, you will be getting double the energy and experience.

"Two of you will require more space." Answer: If we cannot find space that is not being used, we will share.

"How will I know whom to call?" Answer: Either one of us.

Don't let them get you down. Changes are made, pilot programs[8] are instituted, and many of the people in charge of making decisions are able to see beyond their noses. As Harry S. Truman is said to have remarked, "When the facts are known, reasonable men will not disagree."

You know the people you are dealing with better than I do. There are several ways of approaching those who will be making the decision to institute the plan. You may want to either start at the top if it is appropriate or go to the person to whom you report. Try to find someone with a daughter or wife in the same situation. They tend to be the most receptive. You may want to start the ball rolling by bringing up the subject informally, just to test the waters and ferret out possible objections. You can then write up a brief memorandum, sketching out what you have in mind and addressing these objections. Sketch out only the basics because you do not want to box yourself in. If you are the first one in your organization to ask for this arrangement, you will want to keep all doors open. You may not have even identified your future partner. Remember that very important rule of KISS—Keep It Simple Stupid.

Here is something you might adjust to fit your own situation:

MEMORANDUM TO:
FROM: ——— and ———
RE: Flexible Work Project.

8. Calling an innovation a pilot program makes it easier to accept. For some reason people equate the phrase with a hot-air balloon that rises, floats gently above the trees, and comes to rest in someone else's back yard.

We have been working in this organization for many reward-ing years and hope to be able to continue for a long time.

Recently, our family responsibilities have increased to the point where we do not feel that we are being totally fair to you or to them. The two of us have discussed a form of job sharing arrange-ment that we think would bring together our joint experience and energies in a way that would increase our value to this fine organi-zation while managing our family responsibilities.

Some of the details have not yet been worked out, but the ba-sic plan would be that:

1. We would divide the work week, one of us being here at all times.
2. We would divide the salary in accordance with the time spent, but both of us require (health insurance/life insurance/ etc.).
3. We would arrange for both regular and emergency communi-cation so that any information or instruction given to one is transmitted to the other. We intend to operate as a single unit.
4. We will take full responsibility for communication between ourselves and guarantee that information will not have to be repeated, nor will efforts be duplicated. The objective would be to work so closely together that people (clients/customers, etc.) will think of us as one person. We believe that this plan will be of enormous benefit to everyone concerned, and we are committed to its success.

Please let either of us know if you have any ideas about this proposal. In the meantime, we will be working out some of the de-tails and plan to prepare a more detailed memorandum sometime next month.

With this memorandum you have given yourself an opening wedge. You are not asking for an answer—yet—but if the person addressed is unalterably opposed or has any definite thoughts about the plan, he or she is under an obligation to speak up. In law we say that when there is a duty to speak silence is consent.

Within whatever time period you have established, either call or write with further details or any changes that you think might be necessary. Just try to keep things fluid for as long as you can.

It is clear that flexibility is the key ingredient in this as in any other program that involves working together. In this arrangement it is vital that both parties keep an open mind on the details and be prepared to make adjustments as time and experience dictate.

The benefits of this arrangement over part-time work is that the participants are self-selecting and the employer is relieved of the job of filling in the other part. In the part-time work situation, you might not know who will be doing the other part and might get stuck with someone whose bad work reflects, or is blamed, on you.

The idea of job sharing did not originate with me and might have had its roots in the 1930s Depression. Examples exist in work as varied as *Director of Legislation, Manager of Office Services, Probation Officer, Anesthesiologist, School Teacher,* and *Tax Analyst.*[9]

9. See *The Job Sharing Handbook,* by Barney Olmsted and Suzanne Smith, 1996 edition. This handbook, originally published in 1973, is available from New Ways to Work, 785 Market Street, Suite 950, San Francisco, CA 94130–2016. The authors go so far as to suggest that the prospective partners can submit a joint application for jobs previously held by a single person.

# XI
# Don't Say That!

Our usual method of communication with each other is by language, either written or oral. There are people who claim that they can interpret body language, but I consider that to be subjective and not very reliable.

We tend to exercise more discretion when writing. The written word can be changed before it is entrusted to the United States Post Office or alternative methods of delivery or before you strike that send key on your PC. But once you have said it, it is out there for good or evil, and you may not get a chance to elaborate if the person has already left in disgust or hung up.

It is difficult enough to be certain what words themselves mean, but there are certain ones that are bound to disrupt your working relationships.

Here are some examples:

"It's a no brainer." What do you mean a "no brainer"? Everything is a brainer. That's why the brain is there—to be used, and as often as possible. Do not give this advice; it sounds as if you are trying to put something over on someone. If you are on the receiving end of this saying, don't place all your trust in this person who is saying it. Make sure you check out everything, especially the speaker.

"If I tell you this, you must swear never to repeat it." You are just wasting your breath. It's probably general knowledge by now.

"This isn't my station." Then what are you doing here?

"Please call back later/tomorrow/when what's his name is

in." Only if I can't find some other company to give my business to.

"I don't know." This is an incomplete sentence. The complete sentence is "I don't know right now, but I will find out and let you know. Please tell me where I can reach you."

"My mother/husband/wife won't let me." Freely translated this really means that you do not want to do it, and you haven't the guts to say so. More importantly, you are not fooling anyone. This excuse should only be used by children who find themselves in a group that has just voted to burn down the school house with the principal in it.

"We have always done it this way." This is another example of an incomplete sentence. The complete sentence is: "We have always done it this way because . . ." If you cannot finish the sentence, do not use it.

"How old are you?" "What do you weigh?" "How much does your spouse earn?" These questions, unless required for medical or legal purposes, should not be asked, simply because they make liars of us all. Sometime ago I came across an opinion from a Southern court (where else?) that said that a woman who lied, while under oath, about her age, weight, or husband's salary was not guilty of perjury.

# XII
# More Worlds to Conquer

After he conquered Asia Minor, Syria, Egypt, Babylonia, and Persia, Alexander the Great was said to have cried because there were no more worlds to conquer. But in the fourth century, he could not have dreamed of all the worlds to be conquered and discoveries to be made. We only think we have seen everything. Every day something new comes on the market that we seem not to be able to live without. And there are more to come. Personally, I think the following products would make it easier for all of us to live and work together.

Why don't they. . . .

Make a lamp that doesn't need to be plugged into a socket. All my sockets are inconveniently spaced along the wall and my need for light is generally in the middle of the room. This requires either drilling holes in the floor or lighting from above. There must be a way to provide illumination without setting the place on fire.

Manufacture a really small umbrella that fits into a pocket or purse. And while they are at it, change the shape so that it covers me without poking everyone within a yard on every side. If it isn't too much extra trouble, I would also appreciate it if the umbrella hooked on so that I had at least one hand free to wipe my nose.

Sell windows with built-in shades so that I do not have to hang sheets on all the windows until the curtains are selected, sewn, and installed in the new house.

Combine shower heads with dryers so I can dry both me and the shower walls.

Develop grass that never grows more than a specific length, but will reemerge if pulled out. How hard can that be? My eyebrows already do that.

Produce a lamp that turns itself off when I close either my book or my eyes.

Install a remote on the vacuum cleaner that will raise the furniture so that I can clean under it or recover missing items hidden by children or pets.

Make automobile tires that turn sideways so that the car just slides into the parking space.

Build a road that would allow me to designate my exit or street and buzz me when I was a few miles away. Just think of the improvement to the environment, reduction in accidents, and gas savings. This is not an impossible dream. There have been reports of automated highways and computer-operated vehicles from the days of the 1939 World's Fair in Flushing, New York. More recent information indicates that modifications can be made to existing highways and automobiles at reasonable cost to the drivers and public.[10]

Print books with very thin paper that thickens when exposed to the air.

Manufacture knives that become blunt when in contact with human skin.

Manufacture a gadget that can be used to insert and remove contact lenses without sticking your finger in your eye.

Put back those side vent windows in automobiles. I notice that they kept them in trucks.

Manufacture soft, disposable bed linen for those terrible times when we are caring for someone very ill.

Print all books with built-in bookmarks (ribbon is fine). It

10. "High-Tech Travel Gets a Road Test," by Todd S. Purdum, *New York Times,* August 7, 1997.

hurts me to dog-ear pages, and I can never find the bookmarks that they just stick in the bag when you buy the book.

Redesign those telephones that combine talking, listening, and dialing functions in one small hand-held instrument. The problem arises when I reach one of those automated services that requires punching numbers along the way. Maybe they think that my finger has an eye on it and can fit in between my cheek and the telephone.

Install built-in headrests in bathtubs.

Produce an invisible sound barrier large enough to shield me and my table companions from the ubiquitous amplified music that impedes all attempts at conversation and flirting. If people cannot talk to one another or even ask for the salt without screaming, there is no sense in trying to arrange convivial seating arrangements.

Install one of those keys (like those on the sardine cans) on the end of the toothpaste tube so that it will stay wound tight and we can get out the last drop.

# XIII
# Keep in Touch

We are constantly exhorted to communicate—with spouses, friends, family, and especially children. Keeping the lines of communication open, we are told, will solve most of our interpersonal problems. I have never been very good at communicating with young children. Have you noticed that they do not really speak the way those little darlings do on television? But I do know that being on speaking terms with grown-ups provides one with a wellspring of information, which would not otherwise be available without the expenditure of much time and effort.

The more people who remember you, return your telephone calls, and are willing to talk to you, the wider and more extensive will be your sources of information. Somebody is bound to know either the answer, where it can be found, or who else might know. Those who hesitate to display their ignorance or are terrified of rejection are missing many opportunities to perform their job efficiently.

We have many ways of reaching out to people. The telephone is fast and handy, but it can be frustrating if you are put on hold or if the answering machine wants more information than you are prepared to impart. I always wonder if my e-mail really got through. I usually wind up picking up the telephone to make sure. My preferred method is the good old-fashioned letter or note. These can be handwritten or typed on your word processor and, despite rumors to the contrary, are generally delivered within a reasonable time after you have entrusted them to the United States Postal Service.

The good thing about real letters in real envelopes is that they make a nice change from all the bills, catalogues, and pleas for your money. Many people do not use this method of communication because they think they are unable to write a decent letter, are unsure of their spelling, and are positive that their handwriting, if analyzed, would show several congenital personality defects.

But these are all excuses. Using a dictionary or the Spell Check function on your word processor will take care of the spelling problem, and I would not worry about your handwriting. Analysis is pretty expensive and is not considered a science. The kind of letters that I am talking about can be short, to the point, and recirculated to various people. Here's the secret: it almost never matters what words you use as long as the stationery is good.

As to the stationery—please pay attention. This is very important. Buy the best you can: 100 percent rag (really 100 percent cotton fiber) and 30 to 40 pound weight. Your full name should be on the top or center if using note paper (called informals), and your address on the envelope, either engraved or printed in thermography (raised printing). If you want to be taken seriously, I would avoid cutesy pictures or drawings. They belong on children's writing paper.

The informals that fold over the top are my favorite form of stationery, and I prefer them to the half-sheets, which require a steady hand and a better spatial sense than I have in order to keep the lines straight. Note paper nicely accommodates three or four sentences and looks as if you would have written more if you had more paper. You start on the first page if your name is on the top, then go on to the third, and from there to the second page. If your name is on the middle of the first page, then start on the third page and continue on the second. In both cases, it is not considered elegant to write on the fourth page. Forget this rule if you have more to say. If you are more wordy than you thought, you cannot use a second informal. You may have to redo the whole thing in a smaller hand to get everything you wanted to say on the paper. If you don't want to rewrite the note, you may just have to skip the whole thing and find another method of communication.

Correspondence cards are useful and favored by men and some women. The really great thing about them is that you are not supposed to write on the back, and there are no second sheets. It looks fine to send them out with only a few lines written.[11]

Now that you have all that fancy stationery and a smooth writing pen,[12] use them to keep in touch with people that you know or would like to know or those that you think might be helpful someday. You cannot go wrong unless you engage in threats or scatological language. Everyone loves mail.

Writing the letter is the last step to keeping in touch. Before you put words down on a piece of paper, you have to figure out where you're going to send that paper. So, the key phase in correspondence is keeping a list of home and e-mail addresses plus telephone and fax numbers. Use a traditional address book, store these numbers on your computer, or carry a portable electronic organizer. Do whatever it takes to keep this list close at hand. Hold on to business cards and personal cards. They are easy to staple into a Rolodex. If you have a business card, give it out freely. Never throw out an envelope with an address on it until you are sure that you already have the address. Always keep a supply of stamps in your desk. If it's inconvenient to go to the post office (and it usually is), you can order them by mail in a postage-free envelope. I find that the stamps actually arrive more promptly than my other mail.

11. An excellent source of information about stationery, with the history of paper and helpful forms and examples of thank you notes, condolence notes, and other social correspondence is *Crane's Blue Book of Stationery,* edited by Steven L. Feinberg and published by Doubleday.
12. I use those inexpensive disposable extra fine point pens. I once bought a really costly pen and I didn't find it any better.

Notes are not the only way to keep in touch with people. Gossip works sometimes. It tends to be a bit unreliable, but it is definitely enjoyable. Probably, your best source of information will come from the company newsletter or the newspapers. They're easy to read, and they put people's names in bold print. You don't even have to read an entire article. You just have to scan the page and look for names of people you know.

If it will not absolutely ruin your day, it is a good idea to glance through the obituaries. Even if you are too young to harbor such morbid thoughts, remember your friends have parents and grandparents. Real mail can brighten a day especially if someone is grieving. Your note need not say more than the acknowledgment of a loss. Be as generous as you can with the character of the dead, and say that you hope time will soften the blow. Once you have written your first condolence note, you can use it for a lifetime.

I have the greatest regard for those who create those clever cards. The ones I like best and use most often are the funny get-well cards. But printed sympathy cards are just too cold for my taste.

One of the easiest and fastest ways to keep in touch is to have a small pair of scissors close by when you read the newspaper and clip and ship. Clip articles or cartoons that will interest or amuse others and ship them out on your stationery, with one of those sticky notes, or with your business card. Make sure that the recipient knows whom it is from. Take an extra minute and jot down a note.

This reminded me of the time when we . . .
Thought you would get a laugh out of this one.
You might be interested in this.
You're getting famous.

Promotions and job changes (when voluntary) are times

when hopes are high and people are thinking kindly about themselves and others. Get in line for the good feelings with a note of congratulations. Again, it need not be a long review of everything that has happened and will happen. Just say that the person deserves the promotion/job and that the company/firm/governmental unit, etc., is lucky to have such a talented person working for it. Make sure that you send this note immediately before disillusion sets in on either side.

Births are another happy time for folks. Even if you do not feel it necessary to send a present, the parents (and grandparents) will be pleased to get a note of congratulations. Printed cards are okay here. After all, how much can you say about a newborn that you have never even met and certainly never spoke to?

If your company has a newsletter, make it a point to mention any favorable item reported about a co-worker to that co-worker. If there is a picture, say that it doesn't do the person justice. People tend to be self-conscious about having their name and photograph published. A comment like this puts people at ease and gives them a real boost.

Don't hesitate to write simply because you have not been introduced. Our mailboxes are filled these days with communications from strangers who may not know our names and call us "current resident." I often write to authors of books that I have enjoyed. They never seem to write back, and I may discontinue this practice. You can get special recognition by writing to someone who has written a letter to the editor. It proves that you read more than the comics. Unless you feel compelled to disagree with what was written, you can always write that the letter was thought-provoking.

Christmas and New Year's cards are a wonderful way to remind people that you are still among the living. Many people go further and call on New Year's Day, or as soon as the effects of the celebration have worn off, to wish their friends well.

It is a special kindness to get in touch with a friend or acquaintance who has run into some trouble. The calamity is the subject of every conversation and may have been given some serious newspaper or television coverage. These are head-pounding, stomach-wrenching times for everyone involved. Neither children nor any others remotely connected to the incident are spared the trauma.

Please remember:

1. Good people sometimes do foolish things.
2. It is not your job to judge.
3. It could be a lie or a mistake.
4. Eventually the whole thing will be forgotten, but your note or call will be remembered, probably because it was one of a very few or the only one.

Write or call if only to say that you are thinking of them. If you do write, keep it a little vague. Nobody is asking for your opinion on the matter. Strong letters of either condemnation or approval have a bad habit of turning up to your embarrassment when all the facts are known or public perception changes.

Now that you have this large circle of talented, educated, knowledgeable friends with whom you have kept in touch and sent letters of congratulations, condolences, etc., you ask, how will it help me in my work?

It will help because opportunities come from the most unexpected sources. The more people you know (and the more recent the contact) the more likely it is that you will get the information you need. Let's look at some possible examples.

1. Your friend at XYZ Company will know or find out the name of the printer who did such a good job printing their last report at that ridiculously low price.
2. The person who has been with your company since the year one will tell you how and why the company lost that big ac-

count. Maybe there are new people over there who were not involved in that debacle.

3. The person to whom you wrote about the letter to the editor might just remember the name of the chairman of the committee you need to contact.
4. Friends, acquaintances, even competitors are fertile sources of referral. Many people, when asked for a referral, find it safer to give several names. You want to be on everyone's list.

Keeping in touch can also aid us in all those other ways that help us do our jobs and maintain family life in a decent and sanitary manner:

1. Your friend on the school board will help you find the person to contact about Susie's transfer papers.
2. Household help, doctors, dentists, plumbers, painters, babysitters, nannies, dry cleaners, etc., are best gotten through recommendation. The nicer you are to the recommender, the better the recommendee.

They can't help you if they do not remember who you are. Someone once said that most of life is just showing up. That's fine if you are already famous and/or easily recognizable. The rest of us must make some kind of impression—preferably favorable.

In times past when women and minorities were rare in certain fields, anyone who finally got in had an advantage. They stood out. This happened to me when I became the first woman partner in the firm and the only woman in the country practicing a specific type of law. That would not be true today.

Even if you can't or won't make yourself noticed by exaggerated garb or mannerisms, there are some things each of us can do to avoid obscurity.

Of course you will always greet those whom you may not have seen in a while by mentioning your name and some identifying phrase, "I'm Susie Smith from ABC Company." Just because you don't know their name is no reason to avoid contact. Just say something innocuous with a pleasant smile. "Haven't we met?" "I'm sure you and I worked on the ———— project." Sometimes you are wrong, but maybe you have made a new friend.

A book that is full of helpful hints and savvy strategies, as well as a fun read, is *How to Work a Room,* by Susan RoAne, Warner Books Edition, 1988.

Cards[13] are handy and everyone hands them out, but if your business or profession is not clear from the name, it is a good idea to identify the area by:

Financial Advisor
Printing
Residential and Commercial Real Estate
All-Occasion Photography
Exotic Dancing

Jim Farley once said that he could recall the first names of 50,000 people. Many people find it difficult to remember the name of a close relative when faced with an introduction, especially after a small libation. It is polite to relieve any possible embarrassment by springing forth with your name, and, if you remember, your relationship to the introducer. For example. "Mary Jones. I was Jane's roommate in college."

You will be grateful to find that you have added names of secretaries, assistants, children, spouses, alongside the names in your Rolodex. It warms my heart and loosens my purse strings when I call my rabbi and he knows the names of my daughter, four stepchildren, their spouses, and my nine grandchildren. Intellectu-

13. Even if you are not in business, personal cards are a really nice touch and add a touch of class.

ally I know it is right there on the computer screen, but emotionally it still works.

Many people are unforgiving if you misspell their names, even if they have altered the usual form or use a nickname. The same is true of pronunciation. It is always safest to ask.[14]

In other words everyone needs a hook!

All those automatic telephone systems have replaced the operator with the cheery voice and soothing tones who usually knew where everyone was and when they would be back. Since most of us are forced to answer our own telephones, it is important to keep your voice as pleasant as possible. Your tone should convey the impression that you are delighted to be called. If it turns out to be the sixth telemarketer in a row, you can revert to whatever tactic you usually employ. Banging down the phone is rude and doesn't help your blood pressure. Pretending an interest is just mean. This wasn't the caller's first career choice. I think of "not interested" and a quick cut-off as being helpful. The sooner I hang up, the sooner the caller can dial someone else who just might be panting to buy 1) $100,000 of stock in a company that he or she never heard of from a stranger who said it was going to be the next takeover target, or 2) lightbulbs at twice the usual price from someone who said he represented emotionally deprived parents whose children refused to visit them just because the maximum security prison was three thousand miles away.

On those days when a cheerful tone is simply beyond endurance, let the answering machine or voice mail take over. You can return the call when you are feeling human again.

Often, we receive calls intended for someone else in the organization. (Wrong numbers do not count for this purpose.) This is when you can sow the seeds of cooperation. The idea is not just get rid of the caller as quickly as possible in a manner that will insure

14. I on the other hand, really do not care as long as you write to me. Spell it Lyle, Leila, Leelah, but don't call me "madam."

no return call, but to increase the likelihood that your organization will prosper and that you will share in the rewards. Try to contact the person intended, take intelligible messages, and make reasonably sure that they are delivered.

Be a bit careful offering to help unless you really know what you are getting into and have nothing else to do for the foreseeable future. I did that once and found myself representing a sweet schoolteacher from Vermont in a domestic relations matter. Her deposition was so steamy that the transcribing secretary quit on the spot. I typed the transcript. I was not convent-raised, but still to this day I do not understand all of what she described.

# XIV

# Bread upon the Waters

One of my favorite people, a man who taught me how to be a lawyer, would urge the lawyers in his department to "cast bread upon the waters." He strongly believed that this was one way to success, and it worked very well. By casting bread upon the waters, he meant lending a hand. For example, if a competing lawyer or firm began to offer clients the same service in the same field in which he was a nationally known expert, he would welcome in the competition, on occasion even teaming up to give the newcomer credibility. This practice was generally appreciated and often led to other engagements.

Things may be a bit more competitive and perhaps less congenial in the law business these days, but it is still a good idea. Nothing is gained by trying to keep competitors out. If they are good, they will get in anyway, and if they are bad, nothing will help. You might as well be cooperative. But that doesn't mean you have to give away all the trade secrets. You are not obliged to hand over your business/customer/clients. Neither praise nor pan your competition. Sometimes the mere growth of an industry will help you get a piece of a larger pie.

Here are other ways to cast bread upon the waters in the hope that it will come back in loaves.

## Make Hay with the Competition

There are very good reasons why many industries locate near one another. They feed on one another; they buy from one another; they learn from one another. Where physical location is not feasible, contact is often maintained through trade shows, conferences, trade associations, and gossip sheets.

People who labor in the same field form a sort of community. They know the good guys from the bad, the skillful from the incompetent, the ethical from the sleazy, the expensive from the cheap, and every degree in between. In other words, they can help you if you play it smart. Making enemies of your competition is not smart. You will just spend valuable time looking over your shoulder, and they will still get you when you least expect it.

First you must know who is doing what, how it is being done, and how much is charged (and presumably collected, although this is not easy to do). There are not many true monopolies left. (They even broke up Ma Bell.) And remember—there are no secrets. Too many times the action you would not take, the job you thought too risky, or too much trouble may be the next hot item, and, to your regret (and embarrassment, since everyone will find out that you were the one who turned down the job), is now being offered to some upstart who didn't know it couldn't be done, wouldn't sell, and cost too much to do.

## New Business

When someone you know goes into business or gets a new job, any help or encouragement you can give will be much appreciated, and, hopefully reciprocated. Be sure to do it early before either success or dismal failure make anything you do irrelevant.

If possible, and your friend's product or service is not an absolute ripoff, make a purchase or a referral. A celebratory lunch, plant, card, or telephone call is a nice gesture, and nicer yet if others see it. The point here is that your friend's status is enhanced by your attention.

## Friends

Someone you know is, or will, run for public office. Support your friends—they may even win. Any campaign costs money. Forget about major media exposure; printing and postage can be a sizable amount. Early in my career, I was advised to contribute to the campaign of any friend or associate despite political affiliation. Small contributions are usually remembered if given early on with encouragement, but if you wait too long, it will cost more to make an impact.

## Volunteerism

This is the modern-day equivalent of joining the Masons or some other organizations where one would be likely to make business contacts. This is not to say that every volunteer is looking for business or professional advantage, but it does happen with some frequency, enough to warrant looking into.

Volunteers are always interesting people, involved in community affairs, and very often have lots of money. Otherwise they would not have the time to devote to nonpaying activities. They fall into several categories:

1. Those who want to run the show. Let them.
2. Those who want it on their curriculum vitae. They come to few meetings and will be glad to talk to you.
3. Those who do a lot of talking, have grandiose ideas, but are to busy to do much work.

4. Those who do the work. Get on their committee.

Start your career as a volunteer slowly. Volunteers always think that other volunteers have all the time in the world, and they will ask you to join other worthwhile organizations. Before you know it, you will be working for causes about which you know nothing. This can be dangerous.

# XV
# More Tricks of the Trade

I do not flatter myself that I am the only one who has learned how to work with people and how to get them to work with me. Some very successful friends have shared their secrets. Here are some of the best.

Host—If guests ask what they can bring, tell them. If it is a small party, invite people by telephone and then send a reminder with the names of the other guests. Yours is not an English country house where guests are presumed to know each other.

Stockbroker—Learn to love rejection. That fifth call is a sale.

Doctor—Listen to the patient; he will tell you what is wrong. Confirm the diagnosis by your examination, and use tests to prove you are right.

Lawyer—Know your client, what he wants, and how you will be paid.

Salesperson—Know where it is, what goes with it, and how it works.

Manager—Fast decisions are not always necessary. Some things get done without you.

Waiter—Tell them how much the Chef's Special, Lobster Stuffed with Truffles, costs before they order it.

Driver—Fill the gas tank and empty the bladder before starting the engine.

Harried Houseperson—Set the table first. They will think that dinner is almost ready.

Fund-raiser—The most successful one I have ever encountered starts out by boasting, with a big smile, that his cause is noble, *and that he has no shame.*

Volunteer—Raise your hand for the first task to be assigned, unless it is to raise money or organize the whole thing. You may get off the hook for the tough ones coming along later.

**All Suggestions Gratefully Received.**